Rookie
Read-About® Science

It Could Still Be a Flower
WITHDRAWN

By Allan Fowler

Consultant
Janann V. Jenner, Ph.D.

Children's Press®
A Division of Grolier Publishing
New York London Hong Kong Sydney
Danbury, Connecticut

Visit Children's Press® on the Internet at:
http://publishing.grolier.com

Designer: Herman Adler Design Group
Photo Researcher: Caroline Anderson
The photo on the cover shows a close-up of a daisy flower.

Library of Congress Cataloging-in-Publication Data

Fowler, Allan.
    It could still be a flower / by Allan Fowler.
        p. cm. — (Rookie read-about science)
    Includes index.
    Summary: Describes a variety of flowers and explains how
and why they bloom.
        ISBN 0-516-21681-3 (lib. bdg.)   0-516-27308-6 (pbk.)
        1. Flowers—Juvenile literature. [1. Flowers.] I. Title. II. Series.
QK653.F68   2001
582.13—dc21   99-057018

Do you have a favorite kind of flower?

Yellow tiger lilies

4

Maybe you like roses.

Roses can be different colors like pink, red, or yellow.

Some roses smell sweet.

Maybe you like sweet William, black-eyed Susan, or Queen Anne's lace. These flowers were named after people.

Sweet William

Black-eyed Susan

Queen Anne's lace

Have you ever seen a morning glory?

This flower opens up, or blooms, in the morning.

In the evening, it closes.

stems

Many flowers grow straight out of the ground on stems.

Some flowers grow on shrubs, such as azaleas (uh-ZAIL-yuhs) or lilacs (LIE-laks).

Azaleas

Lilacs

Other flowers grow on trees, such as magnolias or cherry blossoms.

Magnolias

Cherry blossoms

Some people plant
bulbs to grow flowers.
Hyacinths (HI-a-sinths)
and lilies are flowers
that grow
from bulbs.

Bulb ⟶

Hyacinth

Lily

buds

Before most plants grow
flowers, they grow buds.
Buds are on the stems
of plants.

Many flowers burst out of buds in the spring. Other flowers bloom in the fall.

Asters bloom in the fall.

Most flowers need good soil, sunlight, and water to grow.

A few kinds of flowers can live without soil.

Beautiful flowers called orchids (OR-kids) often bloom high up on trees in rain forests. They get their water out of the air.

Many flowers grow on their own.

We call them wildflowers because people did not plant them.

Wildflowers can be as lovely as the flowers in a garden.

There are so many
wonderful kinds
of flowers.

Enjoy them all!

Words You Know

bulb

buds

rain forest

wildflowers

stems   shrub

Index

About the Author

Allan Fowler is a freelance writer with a background in advertising.
Born in New York, he now lives in Chicago and enjoys traveling.

Photo Credits

Photographs ©: Envision: 29 (Jean Higgins); Peter Arnold Inc.: 21 (David
Cavaonaro), 7 top (Werner H. Muller), 15 (Johann Schumacher), 14 (Clyde
H. Smith), 16, 30 top left (Michel Viard); Photo Researchers: 17 left (George
Bernard/SPL), 12 (Geoff Bryant), 13, 31 right (Alan L. Detrick), 17 right
(Michael P. Gadomski), 6 (Gilbert Grant), 26, 30 bottom right (Richard R.
Hansen), cover, 18, 30 top right (John Kaprielian); PhotoEdit: 22 (Michael
Newman); Superstock, Inc.: 4; Tony Stone Images: 9 (David Carriere),
3 (H. Richard Johnston), 10, 31 left (David Woodfall); Visuals Unlimited:
7 bottom (Derrick Ditchburn), 25, 30 bottom left (K. B. Sandved).